Phantom Trains
and
Haunted Rails
of the U.S.

Clarissa Vazquez

This book is dedicated to ghost enthusiasts and railfans alike; To Doug for sharing his love of both with the world; To Kristin and Donnie for keeping me laughing through the tears; Of course, to my Jacob for his love of trains when he was little and his passion for ghostly things now. I love you forever!

~C.V.

Table of Contents

INTRODUCTION

During my career as an afterlife researcher, I have heard many stories of things that go "bump" in the night. Most are just antiquated legends that have morphed over the years into fantastical tales, guaranteed to raise the hair on your neck. Some are fabricated for entertainment purposes or practical jokes, while others are the real deal – experiences that just cannot be explained by scientific methods. The one thing all of the stories have in common is the audience. Almost everyone loves a good ghost story! As a kid, I used to read "Scary Stories to Tell in the Dark" by Alvin Schwartz, with its harrowing ghostlore and macabre illustrations. From there, I was hooked.

Many years later, while I was on active duty in the U.S. Air Force, I came face-to-face with my first ghostly entity. The base where I was stationed was in the process of converting their hospital morgue into a physical therapy department. Being a low-ranking Airman on the proverbial totem pole, I was tasked with cleanup during the renovation. After returning to the construction area after my lunch break one day, I saw a man standing alone in the gutted room. Dressed in 1970's-era combat fatigues, he was a stark contrast from the camouflage battle dress uniform I was wearing. Clean-cut with a flat-top hair cut, he certainly looked out of place as he stood in the room looking confused. He was three-dimensional, not whispy or transparent. He looked as real as any other living being. From about twenty feet away, I asked if there was something I could help him with. He looked at me, then turned and walked through a cinder block wall.

Amazingly, I was not the least bit frightened by this experience and I placed an excited phone call to my mother that night when I returned to my barracks. From there, I read every book I could get my hands on. This was before the introduction of reality ghost-hunting TV shows and the Internet was in its infancy, so I was limited to the literary works of paranormal pioneers such as Hans Holzer and Ed Warren.

My thirst for knowledge was unquenchable and I began amateur investigations, utilizing tools like Polaroid cameras and analog tape recorders. Eventually, cemetery romps led to checking out the homes of friends and family. Ultimately, I was called upon to investigate businesses and homes of people I had never met. These people were frightened and seeking help from anyone who would listen without judgment. This led to a partnership with my very good friend, Chade Abplanalp and together we founded the Colorado Coalition of Paranormal Investigators (CCPI) in 2004.

Over the decades, I have had the immense pleasure of researching and investigating many notoriously haunted locations in the United States. I have worked alongside some of the biggest names in the industry and have made many friends along the way, so why trains?

In 2001, I was blessed with a son. He was, and still is, the light of my life and I love him more than anything – living or departed. When he was a toddler he was fascinated, if not obsessed, with anything having to do with locomotives, rail cars or tracks. To this day, I can still hear his small voice squeal with delight at the sight of railroad activity, "Mommy, a choo-choo train!" Even as a teenager, he still enjoys seeing trains although they don't seem to be as exciting for him as they once were.

Many years later, I met my first "railfan". These are people who stand along train tracks at all hours of the day and night with cameras in hand, waiting for a train to come along. For most, it doesn't matter what train is careening past them, although a rare locomotive will certainly get their juices flowing. There are several websites and blogs for railfans that contain photos, video and stories from their adventures.

I wanted to incorporate my love for ghosts with my son's and friend's love for trains as a Christmas present. I scoured the Internet looking for just the right book and found that there weren't any non-fiction pieces that fit my criteria. That day, I decided to combine my writing talents with the other two passions in order to create the book that you are currently reading. "The phantom train phenomenon has often been said to be confined to the United States and Britain, suggesting it may have some specific cultural significance as folklore. However, international cases, though rarer, do exist" (Durwin). There are so many stories out there about haunted railways, with some only getting a nod here or there. Others are information-plentiful, but one thing remains the same: whether you're a paranormal investigator or railfan, this book will have you wanting to grab your camera or EMF meter to check these places out for yourself!

It is my sincere desire that ghost enthusiasts and railfans alike enjoy this book, as I have enjoyed researching and writing it! All aboard!

ARIZONA

Shadow Train

In the heat of the Arizona desert, near the Dragoon Mountains, an unidentified prospector was traveling to Dos Cabezas to seek his fortune. His burro had already died from heat and dehydration and the prospector was nearing death himself, but he was determined to continue to the nearest town or watering hole.

As is the case with many tales of this nature, the prospector collapsed from the searing heat. He reportedly thought of his mother and "the sorrow [she] would feel when he did not return home from his wanderings" (Schlosser, 2004). Defeated, he slipped into unconsciousness.

Some time later, the prospector was awakened by the sound of a train whistle. Confused and delirious, he dismissed the sound as a hallucination and resigned himself to the concept of dying alone in the desert. As he lay cooking in the desert sun, he remembered a conversation he'd once had with an old timer about a shadow train that was said to appear from nowhere in the flats north of the Dragoons. There were no tracks in the area and the nearest town was many miles away. The old timer claimed to have seen the train himself – and that it disappeared into the distance after speeding past him.

As the prospector reminisced over the conversation, the sounds of a train grew louder and in the distance he thought he saw a steam engine heading straight for him. The approaching locomotive was black as pitch with a shining yellow light and two rail cars in tow.

The prospector stared in disbelief as the train's whistle blew again, much louder this time. He feared the train would hit him, but he was too weak to move out of its path. The steam locomotive raced toward him, but stopped just feet away.

A conductor and another man exited the train and walked toward him. They gently picked him up and brought him to one of the cars. The Prospector asked the men for water just moments before losing consciousness again. He awoke to the feeling of water being splashed on his face. Opening his eyes, he saw a lawman with a water pitcher.

"Fellow found you nearly dead about five miles out of town," the sheriff answered laconically.

"What town?" asked the young prospector cautiously, visions of shadow trains and jolly conductors in his head.

The sheriff looked at him strangely. "That sun sure must have messed with your head, son, if you can't even remember where you was headed," said the sheriff. "You're in Wilcox, Arizona."

"It's a stop on the train, then?" he asked hesitantly.

"Train? There ain't no train around for miles," said the sheriff. "You'd better have some more

water and rest a bit. That sun's nearly sent you
loco!" (Schlosser, 2004).

Eventually, tracks were laid in the area of Wilcox, Arizona, but
people still report the ghost train speeding through the area of the
flats during the heat of the day.

COLORADO

BRIDGE OVER KIOWA CREEK

On May 21, 1878 a Kansas Pacific freight train was traveling eastbound when it went off of a bridge that had been damaged by a flash flood. While the freight cars were located in the creek, the actual locomotive was never *officially* retrieved. Clive Cussler believes it was "dug up in the dead of night and towed to Kansas City, where it was rebuilt and renumbered" (Cussler). According to the Shadowlands Haunted Index:

> [Three people] died. [People report] seeing or hearing a ghost train passing by (Shadowlands).

Could these reports be the result of Geographic Psychic Trauma?

> When one or more spirits are believed to inhabit the scene of their violent death, it is known as Geographic Psychic Trauma (GPT). The spirit is believed to be imprinted (for lack of a better term) on the land or building where their life energy left their physical body. What researchers are learning is that the more tragic and violent the death, the more likely it will be for some form of spirit energy to remain directly connected to the place where they died. (Vazquez. 40)

If the theory surrounding GPT is true, then the reports of the ghost train could be the result of the three passengers whose lives were so quickly and violently taken during the accident.

LAST DOLLAR INN

Cripple Creek, Colorado was a mining destination after Bob Womack discovered gold there in 1890. In 1896 three fires destroyed most of the businesses and several homes, ending the boom. The people who chose to stay rebuilt the buildings using brick instead of the traditional wood of that era. Today, Cripple Creek hosts legalized gambling in the historic gold rush-era buildings.

The Florence and Cripple Creek Railroad (F&CC) was a 3 ft narrow gauge railroad running northward from junctions with the Denver & Rio Grande Railroad at the mill towns of Florence and later moved to Cañon City, on the banks of the Arkansas River, up steep and narrow Phantom Canyon to the Cripple Creek Mining District, west of Pikes Peak. Started in 1893, it was the first railroad to reach the new, booming mining district from the "outside world"; as a result it earned substantial profits in its first years. The railroad hauled people and goods into the mining district, and ore concentrates from the mines south for milling in Florence or transfer to the D&RG for milling in Pueblo (Ghost Train).

Even though the train route went through Phantom Canyon, there are no reports of any accidents involving trains, nor is there any ghostlore lending to the canyon's name. The narrow gauge is still in operation during the summer months for tourists and railfans to enjoy.

Located at 315 East Carr Avenue, the Last Dollar Inn was built in 1898 and renovated in 1995. It became a bed and breakfast in 1996. Reports of ghostly activity abound in the building, but one of the most perplexing reports is that of a ghost train. According to Odd Places, Travels, and Spooks of Mile High: "Several guests have heard a noisy phantom train while staying in the back rooms, there is a train in Cripple Creek but it only runs during the warmer summer months [sic] not during the winter when this phenomena is most often heard…[the] mysterious ghost of a train conductor is sometimes seen in the living room…" (Odd Places).

Had there been a railroad accident or some other disaster involving a locomotive or rail cars, one could attribute this phenomena to GPT however, since no reports of such events exist, we are left to ponder the reason for the phantom train reports.

DREAD 107

The ghost of a steam locomotive haunts the Denver & Rio Grande Railroad tracks between Gunnison and Grand Junction, Colorado. At the turn of the 19th century, train engineers avoided that specific engine, which they called "Dread 107". The locomotive was attributed to the deaths of many people.

The Black Bridge Spanning the Gunnison River in Grand Junction, CO

By David Canady

Courtesy of Historic American Engineering Record, Library of Congress, Call number HAER COLO, 39-GRAJU, 2-5.

During its early operations, Engineer Bill Duncan drove the train over a trestle that had been washed out, killing several crewmembers and passengers. Later, Engineer Godfrey drove it into a large boulder – killing dozens more. Three months later, with Engineer Bratt at the controls, it encountered an avalanche in the Black Canyon "killing her quota of mortals for the month" (Martin).

In 1909, the railroad finally demolished the 107, but its whistle can still be heard along the Gunnison River, primarily near Crystal Creek but also at the junction of the Gunnison and Colorado Rivers. Today, ghost enthusiasts flock to the area hoping to catch a glimpse of Dread 107 or hear the sound of its ghostly whistle.

MYSTERY ON MARSHALL PASS

Most phantom train accounts come from witnesses near tracks where accidents have occurred. Occasionally however reports come from active trains and their crewmen. One of the most famous reports comes from Marshall Pass, Colorado.

Looming at over 12,000 feet above sea level, the Denver & Rio Grande Railroad narrow gauge tracks on Marshall Pass served as the main passenger route from

**Marshall Pass D&RGR c. 1890
by William Henry Jackson**

Courtesy of Southern Methodist University, Central University Libraries, DeGolyer Library.

Salida to Gunnison, Colorado from 1881 to 1955 (Skinner). Engineer, Nelson Edwards was tasked with the safe operation of the Marshall Pass route. Nelson was an older gentleman and experienced at the helm of the locomotive.

On a chilly spring night in 1889 Nelson noted how "the silence was deeper, the [canyon] darker, and the air frostier than usual" (Skinner). There had been a warning earlier about potential problems with the track and a bridge so the old engineer was extra cautious. Reaching the summit and beginning its descent,

Nelson received a signal to stop the train. As he applied the brakes, he heard the whistle of another train in the distance.

Confused, the conductor of the train entered the engine from the passenger cars to inquire about the emergency stop. The engineer asked why the signal to stop had been given, but the conductor insisted he gave no such signal. As the whistle of the other train grew louder, it was made clear that they needed to resume their journey quickly or collide with the fast-approaching freight train behind them.

> Here is where the story changes, depending on sources. According to the story in the Rocky Mountain News, published in May 1889, Edwards pulled the brake, fearing the worst, and rode through a crowd of 10-12 ghostly men who were fixing the track, and after Edwards' train had gotten through, the [following freight train] hit the broken track and went over the side of the cliff, vanishing as it did so.

> The other account has the following train lifting above Edwards' train and going over the side as the crew watched (Keipp).

The one thing both versions of the tale have in common is the mystery writing in the frost of the engine window when the train reached its destination, *"A frate train was recked as yu saw. Now that yu saw it yu will never make another run. The enjine was not ounder control and four sexshun men wor killed. If yu ever run on this road again yu will be recked"* (Skinner).

The crude message was enough for Nelson Edwards to resign that very day and take a job with Union Pacific. Crews from D&RGR searched the area, but found no sign of an accident and no engineers have reported seeing the phantom train on Marshall Pass since that fateful night in 1889.

TRACKSIDE BEAUTY

Late night runs are common in the rail industry. Tales abound of strange and sometimes supernatural events. The route from Timpas to Thatcher, Colorado holds one such tale.

The train rumbled around him as he adjusted the throttle. The night shift was always the toughest, in the engineer's mind. He had rumbled through Timpas a few minutes ago and was on his way to Thatcher. Not a bad stretch of road, and there was no better train in the entire Atchison, Topeka & Santa Fe Railroad.

He stretched a bit and yawned, trying to stay alert. And then he gasped. The lights had picked up the figure of a beautiful woman with long red-gold hair and wonderful blue eyes standing near the tracks. Too near! He sounded his horn to warn her away. And then he realized that the light was shining right through her. She was a ghost!

She stepped into the center of the track, laughing and beautiful. She disappeared seconds before the train rushed through her. And then she was there, in the engine cab next to him. The scent of roses filled the air. He stared at the ghostly vision, bewitched by her beauty. With an enticing smile, she wrapped ghostly arms about his neck and kissed him. [Then she] was gone.

Dazed (and disappointed!), the engineer finished the run to Thatcher in a trance, completely forgetting to stop at the station. The fireman had to pour water on his head to snap him out of it.

The engineer decided not to tell anyone about the ghost, fearing for his job. But he was plagued by [curiosity]. Finally, he confided the story to a close friend who was a fellow engineer. To his surprise, the friend had heard about the ghost before. The ghost's appearance on the train was by no means uncommon. No one knew who the woman had been in life. But she always appeared on that stretch of track after dark, beckoning to the men on the railroad crew with a bewitching smile. Sometimes, said his friend, sometimes she would come right onto the train!

"Better not tell your wife about it," his friend advised.

The engineer never did (Schlosser).

Was the beauty on the tracks a specter determined to catch a ride with the passing trains? Perhaps she is the residual energy form of a woman who lost her life on or near the tracks. No records can be located to confirm this theory although historical records were not kept as meticulously as they are today.

GEORGIA

DOWNTOWN DALTON RAILROAD

Local legends tell of Native American Chief Red Bird who died after being thrown off his horse during a race in the area of Dalton, Georgia. He is said to be buried where the tracks currently lay. "Train crews have reported strange lights around the bend of Crown Cotton Mills, and there have been many strange car accidents along the tracks [presumably] caused by the angry Chief" (Haunted Places).

Stories of angry spirits such as Red Bird are actually quite common. Not because of the spirits themselves, but because of the circumstances. Ghostlore is full of tales of vengeful Native American spirits whose eternal slumber has been disrupted by the disturbance of burial grounds, being initially interred in a disrespectful manner, or being buried outside of their customs.

Investigators and Native Americans tend to disagree as to whether a solution for these spirits can be achieved. Some believe that the spirits can be "crossed over" either by communicating with them using a psychic medium or by rectifying their burial situation. Others believe the damage has been done and the spirits will remain earthbound eternally.

Regardless of the circumstances, with the case of Red Bird, because so many incidents have been attributed to his spirit, caution should be exercised when attempting to research or interact with the Chief.

ILLINOIS

GHOST TRAIN OF CHICAGO

On September 30, 2013 a Blue Line train made its way through the Forest Park train yard with no one at the controls. The train was scheduled for repairs and had been parked for a week before heading east on a westbound track for nearly a mile, climbing a hill, and striking another train at Harlem Station where thirty people were injured.

The incident is unlike any "veteran city rail workers say they have seen" (Hilkevitch). Several safeguards were in place to prevent incidents such as this, but none of them stopped the runaway train. Robert Kelly, the president of the CTA Rail Worker's Union, stated he'd never seen an incident like this in 27 years and called it a "great concern" considering "we have [people] working in these yards 24 hours a day, seven days a week" (Hilkevitch).

Even stranger was the malfunction of the cameras that were trained on the section of yard where the train had been parked. Further, no one saw anyone leaving the train after it hit the other at Harlem Station. Most rail yards utilize supervisory control and data acquisition (SCADA) systems to remotely control equipment. The Chicago Transit Authority implemented their SCADA system in 2009, which included video surveillance.

One theory was that the SCADA at the train yard had been hacked, allowing an outside source to control the train unbeknownst to the workers at the rail yard. "As a precaution, the

Federal Joint Terrorism Task Force is also involved in the investigation, a law enforcement official said" (Hilkevitch).

It was later determined that the incident was not caused by ghostly activity, as most workers suspected, but by human error.

> Two CTA electrical workers have been fired and two other employees suspended as a result of a collision in September between a "ghost train" that traveled on its own for almost a mile after leaving a West Side rail yard and struck a Blue Line train stopped at the Harlem station, transit officials said Friday.

> The primary cause of the bizarre accident on Sept. 30 has been attributed to a CTA switch worker leaving the four-car train in a powered-up mode while it was in storage at the Forest Park rail yard, according to investigators with the National Transportation Safety Board. Electricity was running to the propulsion system, lights and other equipment.

> Proper procedures to prevent rail cars from moving require retracting the electric coupler buttons to prevent an electrical connection between the cars and disconnecting the batteries,

officials said.

About 30 passengers on the Blue Line train suffered minor injuries when their train was hit head-on by the runaway train.

The two electrical workers were fired for using improper techniques to clean an electrical junction box on one of the cars of the runaway train and for allowing water to enter electrical components, the CTA said.

"The improper techniques were one of a number of circumstances that the CTA has determined contributed to the incident," CTA spokesman Brian Steele said.

The switchman who failed to power down the train, and also violated CTA rules by not notifying a supervisor that the train was still receiving power, was suspended without pay for three days, the CTA said.

The president of the CTA rail workers union first disclosed the suspension of the switchman on Thursday and charged that the CTA used the employee as a scapegoat after the NTSB investigation found that the CTA routinely left out-of-service trains with the power on and the brakes not fully engaged to prevent movement. The CTA disputed the NTSB finding, but it immediately made changes in procedures.

A CTA supervisor in charge of rail car yard cleaning was suspended without pay for two weeks, the CTA said Friday. The exact reason for the suspension was not immediately provided, although the discipline was related to the crash.

One thing remains certain, the incident of the Chicago "ghost train" will remain in the memory of rail workers for a very long time!

TUESDAY MORNING SPECIAL

Every Tuesday morning at approximately 3:30, an invisible train is said to make a run through Elmhurst, Illinois. "If you go to the tracks at that time you will hear the train and feel the vibrations but you won't see it" (Ghosts of America). The ghost train of Elmhurst is believed to be the result of a train wreck in the area. "During a 12 month period between 1992 and 1993, Elmhurst suffered 3 fatal collisions involving trains" (Elmhurst). Could the Tuesday Morning Special be a result of those collisions? Perhaps those collisions enhanced the energy that was already there from a previous train wreck?

Given the consistency and regularity of the Tuesday Morning Special, it is more than likely residual energy resulting from GPT. We have already looked at GPT and the potential causes for it, but what is a residual haunting?

> By literal definition, residual is the residue of something from the past. In this case, the spirit of someone or something that was once living. Residual hauntings almost never interact with the living and frequently replay the same moment in time over and over…There is very little that can be done in residual cases other than study them because the phenomenon does not appear to be conscious or aware of their surroundings. (Vazquez. 25)

Investigators should exercise caution when attempting to investigate locations where train tracks are live, as the potential for an actual train coming down the tracks is very real.

LINCOLN'S FUNERAL TRAIN

There are many tales of the funeral train that carried the body of Abraham Lincoln retracing its journey from Washington D.C. to Springfield, Missouri. The most frequent sightings are in Springfield itself.

President Lincoln's funeral train departed Washington, D.C., on April 21, 1865 at 12:30 p.m., carrying the bodies of the President and his son, William Wallace Lincoln, as well as several dignitaries. "Willie was [originally] buried in Oak Hill Cemetery in Georgetown...He was re-interred at Oak Ridge Cemetery in Springfield, Illinois on September 19, 1871, alongside the remains of his father and his brothers, Tad and Eddie" (William Wallace Lincoln).

The funeral train retraced the route Lincoln had made to his inauguration after being elected. Several stops were made along the way where the President's body would lay in state. Thousands of mourning citizens flocked to view him at each stop. The train finally arrived in Springfield on May 3, 1865.

The funeral train consisted of nine cars, including a baggage and hearse car. Eight of the cars were provided by the chief railways over which the remains were transported; the ninth was the President's car, which had been built for use by the president and other officials, contained a parlor, sitting room, and sleeping apartment, and had been draped in mourning and contained the coffins of Lincoln and his son. Different locomotives were used on different stretches of the trip. The train was preceded [10 minutes ahead] by a pilot locomotive and one car to see that the track ahead was unobstructed (Funeral and Burial).

The "funeral train was dubbed 'The Lincoln Special' [and the President's] portrait was fastened to the front of the engine above the cattle guard" (History.Com). The last of twenty different locomotives tasked with pulling the funeral train, the "Old Nashville", a steam locomotive, was never permitted to travel faster than twenty miles per hour while carrying the body of the President, by order of the U.S. War Department. The Old

The "Old Nashville" with Lincoln's photo affixed to the cow catcher.

c. 1880's

Nashville was ultimately destroyed in a prairie fire near Minneapolis, Minnesota in 1911 (History.Com). While the spectral train has been spotted in many locations along the historic route, its ghost has been repeatedly spotted on abandoned tracks between Prince Albert and St. Louis – most frequently around the anniversary of his assassination. "The train is said to emerge from a cloud of thick, black fog, towing its dark cars. Its arrival makes the air noticeably heavier and colder to all living souls present" (Davies). The train is reported to "stop watches and clocks in the surrounding areas as it passes" (Ghost Train). There are no sightings of the President or his body on the phantom train, however an American flag-draped casket, guarded by Union soldiers has been reported.

KILLER LOCOMOTIVE

In Champagne County, Illinois sits the town of Tolono. Reports of a ghost train there stir the curiosity of paranormal investigators from around the Midwest. "Every other week the 'ghost train' [arrives] at 1:59 a.m. and leaves at 2:01" (Strange USA). While this is exciting because of the regularity, other details of this train are a bit more disturbing, if not deadly.

Investigators and witnesses report that when the "train" appears, it is a blur of white light accompanied by screams. Some people have been seen walking along the tracks, only to disappear, resulting in missing persons cases (Strange USA). Another report comes from an incident in 1996 when an intoxicated man was seen walking on the tracks. "…witnesses say they saw a bright [light] and the shape of a train runnin' down the tracks and before they knew it he was on the ground [dead] (Haunted). There has even been mention of a ghost conductor associated with the train.

If these events are legitimate, are they the result of a residual or intelligent haunting? An intelligent haunting is the spirit of someone or something that appears to be conscious and can interact with the living. If a residual haunting is an energy imprint with no consciousness, then the disappearances could possibly be the result of an intelligent haunting. Perhaps the conductor of the ghost train in Tolono allows passengers to board, never to be heard from again.

McCORMICK TRESTLE

On Thursday, June 5, 1924, the CB&Q #193 was scheduled to leave Vermont, Illinois at 4:15 p.m. en route to Rushville. A freak storm had created several delays, primarily with the switching. After completing their tasks, Engineer Manvels, accompanied by fireman William F. Zimmerman, sounded the whistle and at 5:57 p.m. the 193 departed for Rushville.

The 193 reached McCormick Trestle which crossed Sugar Creek at 6:05 p.m. (Bybee). The water was rapidly flowing from the earlier storm, but neither Manvels nor Zimmerman saw any danger at the crossing. The engine reached the southwest bank, however, the trestle collapsed under the weight of the twenty-ton engine after being damaged by the raging waters of Sugar Creek.

"Manvels and Zimmerman's souls died when the tender upended and plunged like a cannon ball into the chasm opened by the collapsing trestle" (Bybee). Engineer Manvels was crushed under Mogul 260 #1126 while Zimmerman was thrown from the train, suffering fatal injuries and burns. Zimmerman was able to blow the train's whistle to signal for help before losing consciousness.

The Burlington railroad was eventually abandoned in the 1980's. Bits and pieces of the trestle remain, along with the ghost of the 193. Reports of the single light from the ghost engine are common, along with the lonely whistle of a train still trying to reach its destination.

INDIANA

WHITE LICK CREEK BRIDGE

Between Avon and Danville, Indiana runs White Lick Creek. There is no shortage of ghostly reports for the bridge at this location, as well as legends surrounding the circumstances for these hauntings.

During the construction of the creek's bridge in the 1850's many Irish workers were hired in an effort to keep costs down. They were known for working hard and were willing to work for lower wages. A worker by the name of "Dad Jones" (Southern Indiana Ghosts) is reported to have fallen into the wet cement during the construction of the pylons for the bridge. "He slowly sank into the pylon and the other workers could hear his fists hammering against the wooden sides as he slowly drowned" (Taylor). His body was never recovered. Some speculated it was because it would have cost the railroad too much to destroy the pylon and build another. Leaving the body there gave pause to some of the more superstitious workers.

Another version is that of Henry Johnson "an alcoholic construction worker [who] slipped one night during the building of the bridge and fell into some wet cement, dying there in the lonely night" (Ghost Legends).

Whether it was Dad Jones or Henry Johnson, it is said that you can hear his screams and pounding sounds from inside the pylon, confirmed by rail workers constructing a new bridge in 1906.

Another chilling tale is that of a woman and her child. Stories conflict about her demise. One report claims she "was walking to the doctor's house late one night with her sick baby when she had the bad luck to get her foot caught among the railroad ties on the bridge. Then, disaster struck in the form of a huge locomotive barreling down on them" (Ghost Legends). She, along with her infant child, was hit by an oncoming train. Another report indicates she escaped the oncoming train, but had to jump into the creek with the child in her arms. "She survived, but the baby, falling from her arms, did not. Within a few weeks, the mother died of a broken heart…if you drive under the bridge at night, you might very well hear her screaming for her baby" (Ghost Legends).

An additional story tells of a family traveling in the area on Halloween night. They reportedly had "an accident at the bridge site, and now with a visit on Halloween night you can hear the mother screaming and the baby crying" (Southern Indiana).

The remnants of the original bridge can be found a short distance from the existing bridge that is still used by CSX.

IOWA

THE MAN WITH THE LANTERN

Located Southeast of Des Moines, Iowa the town of Avon reports a ghostly man holding a lantern walking along the tracks. Witnesses say that the man eventually disappears.

KATE SHELLEY BRIDGE

In Boone, Iowa local lore tells the story of fifteen year old Kate Shelley who crawled across a damaged bridge during a storm in 1881 to warn an oncoming train of the danger ahead. It is unclear if she fell from the bridge or was struck by the train, but it is said that her ghost remains on the rails.

The bridge was rebuilt in 1901 and "phantom trains have also been seen and heard" (Haunted Places).

LOUISIANA

THE GHOST LADY OF WEST 7TH STREET

Two stories surround the area of West 7th Street in Lake Charles, Louisiana. The first is the tragic beheading of a woman as she tried to cross the tracks in front of a train. "Folks say her ghost can be seen walking down the tracks" (Haunted Places).

The second story is that of an accident involving a car and a train in the 1950's. The accident killed a family of four where the tracks cross the road leading to a rice factory. "A young girl's spirit has been reported, the feeling of being smothered has been felt, and spook lights have been witnessed" (Your Guide).

Both of these incidents were reported before the 2005 flooding that resulted from Hurricanes Katrina and Rita. No new instances involving ghosts and these tracks have been reported following the hurricane.

MARYLAND

THE HEADLESS BRAKEMAN

Chilling tales of headless brakemen, firemen and conductors fill ghost hunting circles all over the country. The most detailed and verifiable account comes from the Syracuse Sunday Herald, originally printed on July 15, 1894.

> Among the strange stories told of the adventures of railroad men, that of an apparition that is at present haunting the sidings at Calverton, Md., in the form of a headless brakeman is current among the men who run over the road at that point. It is alleged that the spectre is often seen by the trainmen, and that accident or disaster of some kind always follows in its wake. For the fifteen years that it has appeared, it is asserted that it has never failed to be the forerunner of mishap or death on the rail. The ghost is supposed to be the relic of a brakeman who was run over and decapitated by his own train years ago.
>
> John Tremont, when asked if he had ever seen the headless railroader, said he had once, about two years ago, when the train on which he was running was passing Calverton about midnight.
>
> "I was standing on the rear platform of the passenger train," he said. "We were running along pretty slow, as we were nearing the city.

Suddenly, I saw something on one of the tracks to the left of the one we were on, which froze my blood and made the cold shivers run up my spine. I had often heard of the ghost, and it was he, sure enough. The train stopped a little to take on another track, and I had a good look at the phantom. The night was dark and it was raining a little, but I could see the figure perfectly, on account of the lantern he carried. It gave out a bluish phosphorescent kind of a gleam that flickered unsteadily. One minute it would flare up bright, and then pale again, like an arc light does sometimes."

"When I first saw the ghost, he was holding the lantern down with his feet, and the upper part of his body was dim. He was swinging the light backward and forward slowly, as if he was giving the signal to 'back up slow.' Just then our conductor came back to the rear end of the car, where I was. I grabbed him by the shoulder and pointed to the ghost. The light shone bright on his brass buttons, and showed his uniform, but it did not show his face---the head was gone. There was a gory, dripping part of the neck. I had to turn away. The conductor grabbed hold of the iron guard of the platform, and said, in a sort of choking whisper: 'Good God, Jack, that means some kind of warning for us.' When I turned around the ghost was gone."

"We were pretty badly broken up over what we had seen: all the more so because we had often heard that when the spook was seen something bad always happened. Tom Spofford, our conductor, was superstitious to begin with, and he was worried nearly to death over it. He thought he was going to be killed, but the lightning didn't strike him. The warning was intended for our engineer, for he was killed the day after, between here and Philadelphia, by falling from the side of old No. 697, while he was walking along the side of the boiler. He was taking his train along at a clipping rate, when he took a notion to go outside and oil the piston 'strike.' Ike McHenry, the fireman, saw him fall over the side. When they slowed up and went to hunt for him they found him lying in a ditch along the track with his neck broken. That's the first and last time I ever saw the headless brakeman, and I hope I may never see him anymore."

At this juncture the two men went off duty, but told the reporter about an old engineer, who, they said, could tell all about the ghost.

"Old Jim McManus was running on the road when the brakeman was killed, and he is full of the story. He knows how the man was killed, what his name was, and everything connected with the business," they said, and from him was learned a story which he vouches for as being strictly true in every particular, and which is corroborated by others. McManus lives on McHenry street. He has not been on the road now for several years, as he is so crippled up with rheumatism that he never gets out of the house except on warm, sunshiny days. At such times it is his delight to visit the depots and other places where engineers and other railroad men congregate, to talk over subjects concerning his former occupation. He is especially fond of talking of the headless brakeman, and avows that he has seen him on several occasions. He was acquainted with the man whose spirit the spook is supposed to represent.

"He was a brakeman when he was killed," he said, "and had risen from the place of train boy. His name was Thomas Murphy, and the boys all called him 'Toper Tom,' for the only fault with him was that sometimes he'd get drunk. He was a jolly fellow and the boys all liked him. That's the way he kept his job for so long, for they wouldn't give him away to the superintendent. If it hadn't been for that he would have been 'dancing on the carpet,' as we call being brought up before the boss, more than once for his fondness for liquor. He stopped drinking all of a sudden and never touched a drop for over a year. He was a nice looking fellow. First he was brakeman on a freight, and then he got promoted to a passenger. This seemed to get him started again. He couldn't stand prosperity or something, and he got worse than he'd been before. All of his friends warned him to stop, but it had no effect on him at all. When they'd tell him that he'd get killed if he didn't look out, he'd only laugh and tell them if he did his ghost would come back and let 'em know when anything bad was going to happen, so that they could be on the lookout.

"He told the truth, for he was killed not long after, and his ghost certainly did come back. It happened this way; I had the run with No. 67 Western ex press, and Murphy was brakeman on the same train. He got some whiskey at Harrisburgh and kept getting drunker and drunker on the run back to Baltimore. The conductor was a friend of his, and he went to him and told him he'd better turn in and go to sleep, but Tom only laughed, and said he was all right. He got kind of ugly, too, and stubborn like, so nothing could be done with him. We were behind and were due in Baltimore about 12:30 at night. I had instructions to stop at the sidings out at Calverton, as a car had to be left there."

"When we got there nothing would do Tom Murphy, but that he'd got to open the switch and let the car go on the siding. The conductor didn't want to let him do it, but he appeared to have sobered up a good deal, and was so stubborn about it that he was let do it just to humor him. The car was put on the siding all right, and we had just started again when the bell rang to stop. I stuck my head out of the cab window to see what was wrong. I saw a crowd gathered about midway of the train with lanterns. I got out and went back. Everybody was standing about the body of poor Murphy, with the head cut off as clean from the trunk as if it had been done with a razor. Nobody knew how it happened, but he must have fell down between the bumpers some way."

"It was some months afterward when stories got to floating around that Tom Murphy's ghost was being seen at Calverton about the siding where he got killed. After a year and a month or so had passed I saw him myself. We were making the same run from Harrisburgh as the one that Tom had got killed on. We drew out in the suburbs, runnin' kind of slow. I was lookin' out of the cab window when I saw him just as plain as day. He was standing up holding the lantern in his hand, waving it back and forth. We stopped just opposite where he was standin' to do some shiftin'. He wasn't more than forty feet away. At first he was standin' as if his front was to toe train. I kicked Bill Thompson, my fireman, to look, and when he saw what it was he turned white as a sheet and stood starin' at the thing as if his eyes would come out. We must have watched it that way for fully a minute, when it walked up the track a little way and disappeared. The lantern give out a greenish lookin' light that showed up his clothes just as plain as if it had been in the middle of the day. After he had gone we both spoke to each other about something that struck us as being mighty queer. The uniform he had on looked as if it had been buried in a damp cellar, or some place where it would become all rusty and worn out."

"I told my fireman not to say anything about what we saw for fear the boys would think we were superstitious, and I didn't want them to kid us about it. Did anything happen soon afterward? The same engine with my fireman--I was taking a day off--ran over some farmer and his team out here in Maryland and killed him and his horses deader than doornails. The farmer was drunk, and was going home from some little country town."

"Every time the ghost of poor Tom Murphy has been seen something has happened only a short while after. Why, last fall when those people were killed out here near Bowie Station one night by being run into--it was their own fault--Tom's headless body was seen only the day before. Whenever he comes it's a dead sure thing that somethin' goin' to happen, and it ain't goin' to be long before it does happen, either." (Headless)

Is the ghost of "Topper" Tom Murphy still wandering the tracks of Calverton, warning of impending doom? Is he a railroad tommyknocker or is he more evidence of GPT resulting in an intelligent haunting?

MASSACHUSETTS

BRIDGE LUNCH

During the compiling of stories for this book, I found more information than I had bargained for. Stories of ghost trains are more common than I had anticipated, but are lumped into categories of other paranormal phenomena. Considering the term "paranormal" means something that cannot be explained rationally or by using the scientific method, I had to weed through stories of UFOs, Marian apparitions (sightings of the Virgin Mary), ghost ships and phantom airplanes. There are enough strange tales to fill the Bermuda Triangle!

One of the stories I stumbled upon was that of the Bridge Lunch in Pittsfield, Massachusetts. Located at the corner of North Street and Eagle, the Bridge Lunch was a busy diner, owned by John Quirk.

In February, 1958 Mr. Quirk, along with several customers, witnessed a steam locomotive complete with baggage car and coaches, travel eastbound along the tracks near the diner. He claimed to have observed the train in great detail, to include coal in the tender. Because steam engines had already been replaced by diesel locomotives, Mr. Quirk decided to report the strange event to railroad officials, but was "informed curtly that no train had passed by at that time. Furthermore, officials pointed out, no steam engine had operated on that line in many years" (Durwin).

In March of the same year, the phantom steamer was seen on the tracks again. This time, it was observed by Timothy

Koutsonecolis and Steve Strauss, two diner employees, along with breakfast-goers at 6:30 a.m. The description was the same as the previous sighting: an eastbound steam engine with a baggage car and several coaches.

That was the last *official* sighting of the phantom steamer in the area of North Bridge. Other minor sightings have been rumored, but none of them contain the great detail of the Bridge Lunch sightings. In addition to the steam engine phenomenon of 1958, Joe Durwin notes "a far higher proportion of dead animals under the North Street bridge than under any of the parallel bridges in town" (Durwin). While the dead animal phenomenon is more appropriately categorized under UFO or cattle mutilations, there is no question that Pittsfield is a location to keep on your paranormal radar!

MICHIGAN

TRESTLE OF SCREAMS

In the Lenawee County city of Adrian, Michigan sits an old train trestle, affectionately dubbed the "ghost trestle". " Ghost Trestle is located in rural, southeast Lenawee County on Bailey Rd -- just a few miles off highway M-52 near Gier Rd or you can reach the location by traveling west on Carleton Rd until you reach Bailey. The area is generally low-traveled except for people that live nearby" (Whichter).

In the late 1800's a family was plagued by a fire in their barn. While the husband attempted to put out the fire, the wife and their infant child raced to the nearby tracks in hopes of flagging down one of the many passing trains for help. Unfortunately, she got too close to the tracks and was struck, killing both her and the baby. The husband reportedly died as well in the fire.

"To this day, it is said you are able to go to the trestle and be able to hear the woman and child screaming late at night" (Whichter). It is also speculated that a "portal" to the other side exists under the trestle. Local teens frequent the trestle for a thrill and many have reported hearing the ghostly screams. The majority of the property surrounding the trestle is public, so permission is not needed, although you should take care to advise local law enforcement of your activities in the area to avoid interference during your investigation.

MISSOURI

THE HEADLESS PASSENGER

In the late summer or early fall of 1892, an accident near Dumas, Missouri claimed the lives of over 1,300 people – most of them thrown into the river from the overpass located about ½ mile from the tunnel. One of the victims was a woman who was decapitated in the accident. Witnesses "believe the woman`s head was lost to the river and now she eternally seeks it. She walks in the fall, mostly. When she passes thru you, you will feel like a thousand icicles stabbing thru you" (Train Wreck).

PHANTOM TRAIN

While not much is known about these reports, many people claim to see and hear a phantom train on the tracks leading from Exeter, Missouri to Butterfield. No accidents have been reported in this area.

NEW JERSEY

THE HOOKERMAN

Rumors and legends of the Hook Man have been circulating since the 1950's. Most include a man whose hand had been severed and replaced with a metal hook terrorizing men and women in rural areas. The story of the Hookerman in New Jersey takes a classic legend and puts an exciting spin on it.

The New Jersey Hookerman is reported to have lost his arm in an accident in the early 1900's. It is believed he "worked on the Bartley-Flanders" (Hookerman Lights). The story claims he was either on the train or trying to signal it to stop when he fell and was left unconscious, his arm having been severed by the train. The ghost of the Hookerman has been seen on the tracks, his metal hook holding a lantern as he looks for his missing arm. "In the 1920's and 1930's the Central Railroad of New Jersey, which owned the tracks, had a notation in their employee timetable not to stop for any lantern signals in this area. That's how common the Hookerman lights were" (Tupaczewski).

> Anthony Muller, a science teacher in Mount Arlington, has seen the lights numerous times. "The effect is a bright, rose- to amber-colored light, ball-like or disk-like in shape, with a diameter of about four feet. It seems to be ten to twelve feet above the tracks and moves in one direction, I would estimate at 25 to 40 mph. I was

quite interested in this phenomenon and began some research. Geologists and electrical engineers told me that quartz-bearing rocks, under pressure and stress, produce electrical discharges in what is known as the piezoelectric effect. The railroad tracks may focus this electrical energy into ball lightning or at least something close to it."

In 1976 Vestigia did research on the Long Valley mystery lights. They used a Geiger counter and methane detectors, in addition, four thousand feet of copper was put between the rails, [the detectors] were attached to amplifiers and oscilloscopes. At ten p.m. on November 20 their instruments registered drastic changes as a small but distinct light appeared a foot above the ground and hovered there for about two minutes before disappearing. The team's cameras photographed a pinpoint of light, with infrared photographs that showed more density and light range of the object. The team then turned to geophysical science for an explanation. The geodesic maps of New Jersey revealed a major fault, the Ramapo Border Fault, which runs through Peapack and ends at Indian Point, New York. Since 1962 there have been no less than thirty-three minor earthquakes along this fault. Because quartz-bearing rock produces an electrical charge under seismic stresses and the railroad bed in Long Valley is granite, which is a very good conductor of electricity, a scientific explanation had been reached (Hookerman Lights).

Paranormal investigators have been researching for decades the correlations between geomagnetic disruptions or piezoelectric transmissions and ghostly activity. While it seems Muller and Vestiga's research has debunked the mysterious Hookerman lights, developments in technology and paranormal science may have debunked their debunking:

> One thing paranormal researchers agree upon almost universally is that ghosts are merely some form of energy. There is a two-part explanation for this. The first part being that the human body is comprised of two things – water and energy. When our physical bodies die, the water evaporates, but where does the energy go? Energy cannot be created nor destroyed, so it has to go somewhere! The second part is the fact that energy fluctuations, whether electric, thermal, or magnetic, have been directly attributed to ghostly encounters (Vazquez. 28).

> Under the right conditions, [quartz] can produce
> an electrical charge (piezoelectricity) and
> transmits ultraviolet light waves better than glass.
> It has the physical capacity for retaining light
> energy and small amounts of electricity, so it
> would stand to reason that it might be able to hold
> the energy that could possibly result in a residual
> haunting (Vazquez. 26).

Given the age of the Muller and Vestiga research, combined with the new technology and research of modern ghost hunting, serious researchers shouldn't be too quick to dismiss the mysteries surrounding the New Jersey Hookerman. If the accident resulted in GPT from the severed limb, then it is quite possible that the New Jersey Hookerman might be a legitimate phenomenon! Unfortunately, the property owners feared someone would be injured while looking for the Hookerman, so the tracks were removed in 1977. Despite the tracks being absent, die-hard explorers still venture out to the area in hopes of seeing the famous Hookerman!

EXPRESS TRAIN TO HELL

A popular tale about a ghost train comes from Central Station in Newark, New Jersey. Legend has it that a man, possibly a vagrant, had been loitering in the station for several days, always being chased away by the stationmaster or local police. The man would jump around, shouting at people, "It's coming for me! It's coming for me! If someone asked him who or what was coming, the man would sorrowfully reply, "'I done wrong! I killed a man that cheated me at cards, and now I'm going to pay!'" (Schlosser).

One night the station master saw the man jumping and yelling again. He urged the man to leave before the police arrived, but the man persisted, "'The Express Train for Hell is coming for my soul! You've got to help me.' He broke away from the stationmaster and ran for the door" (Schlosser). At 11:58 p.m., the station master heard the sound of an approaching train. He found it odd because the next train wasn't due to arrive for another seven minutes.

Upon hearing the approaching train, the man jumped onto the platform, screaming. The station master knew by the sound that the oncoming train was traveling too fast to stop at the Newark station. "The train whistle sounded again. A warm rush of air blew against everyone near the platform and the stationmaster heard the roar of an invisible train passing directly in front of him. He heard the hiss of the steam and the screech of flanges against iron rails; he felt the wind whipping [his] hair and [face], but he saw nothing" (Schlosser).

The man screamed as the phantom strain raced by before vanishing into thin air. Checking his watch, the stationmaster saw that the time was precisely midnight. He stared in disbelief down the tracks as other passengers began clamoring around him.

> "Good lord, he was right," the stationmaster murmured to himself. "It did come for him." He pulled out a handkerchief and wiped his sweating, bald head with it.
>
> A trembling man standing nearby approached the stationmaster: "Sir, what was that?" he asked. "Son, I believe that was the Express Train to Hell," said the stationmaster. He shook his head and that seemed to bring him to his senses. "Why don't you go back into the station and pour yourself a drink?" he suggested to the trembling man. (Schlosser).

The stationmaster did his best to calm and quiet the other passengers, telling them that it was just a passing express and the next scheduled stop would be arriving in about five minutes, although there were still whispers among the still-frightened travelers. He then went into his office, poured himself a stiff drink and pondered adding "Express Train to Hell: Midnight" to the station schedule.

Ghostlore is full of stories of spirits interacting with the living, but none are as detailed and mind-boggling as the express train to hell that carried its passenger off that night!

NORTH CAROLINA

TRAIN WRECK OF NORTH CAROLINA

On August 27, 1891 passengers boarded the overnight train in Salisbury, North Carolina bound for Asheville. Sometime around 3 a.m. the sleeping passengers were awakened when the train began bouncing and rocking violently. The train was crossing the Bostian Bridge near Statesville and derailed after the engineer lost control.

The train and its passengers plummeted more than sixty feet into the water. "Twenty-two people were killed that night in the worst train wreck in the history of North Carolina" (Schlosser).

On August 27, 1941 - on the fiftieth anniversary of the wreck, a woman and her car were stranded with a flat tire near the Bostian Bridge. It was late at night and she was feeling somewhat despondent as she sat in the darkness, waiting for her husband to rescue her. In the distance, she heard the sound of an approaching train and its faint light in the distance. "As [the train] raced across the bridge, it suddenly derailed, screaming its way down and down sixty feet and smashed into the creek bed below. The woman was terrified. She ran toward the wrecked train and gazed down into the creek. She could hear the frantic cries and agonized moans of the survivors" (Schlosser).

No sooner did this happen, than her husband and a local mechanic arrived to help her with her car. Shaking and crying, she raced toward them, screaming herself about the wreck and the casualties below. The men ran to the edge of the small canyon and looked down where the woman claimed to have seen the twisted metal and screaming people. All they saw was water. They never saw the train wreckage or the cries of the injured and dying.

To this day, people congregate in the area of the Bostain Bridge during the early-morning hours of August 27 in hopes of seeing for themselves the residual crash, however great care should always be exercised when looking for phantom trains, as people have been injured or killed in their endeavors.

> Shortly before 3 a.m. Friday [August 27, 2010], on the 119th anniversary of the Bostian Bridge train tragedy and at about the same time, between 10 and 12 ghost hunters were on that approximately 300-foot long span.
> They were hoping to hear the sounds of the crash, and perhaps see something.
> Instead, a real Norfolk-Southern train -- three engines and one car -- turned the corner as it headed east to Statesville, about 35 miles north of Charlotte, authorities said.
> The terrified "amateur ghost watchers" ran away, back toward Statesville, trying to cover the nearly

150 feet to safety, said Iredell County Sheriff's Office Capt. Darren Campbell.

All but two made it.

Christopher Kaiser, 29, of Charlotte, was struck and killed, said Campbell.

A woman who witnesses say Kaiser pushed to safety fell about 30 to 40 feet from the trestle and was injured. Her name and condition were not known Friday night. She was being treated at Carolinas Medical Center in Charlotte.

"There was no way out, said Campbell. "They almost made it."

The engineer of the train, which was traveling at its customary 35 to 40 mph, hit the horn and "stopped as fast as he could," Campbell said.

Campbell, 38, is from the area and has heard all the stories, although he said he knows of no one who has ever seen or heard the "ghost train."

On the 50th anniversary of the Bostian Bridge incident, a woman said she witnessed it all again. In 1991, hawkers sold T-shirts and other memorabilia, and there were an estimated 150 people waiting for the train, according to the Charlotte Observer.

There are occasional reports of railroad crossing arms dropping without cause, Campbell said.

The ghost trip on the anniversary has become an annual tradition of sorts.

A woman who did not want to be identified, but who was part of the group of onlookers, told CNN affiliate WCNC, "We were there looking for what people say happened. You hear the train wreck or hear people screaming. We were just watching." Kaiser's mother said the family was too distraught to talk about the incident, WCNC said.

Campbell said most of the ghost hunters, who were from out of town, have been interviewed. Many fled because they were trespassing on railroad property, he said. Campbell said there were no patrols near the bridge early Friday. Although the investigation is continuing, Campbell said the incident appears to be an accident.

At least two blogs that cover the phenomena, N.C. Ghost Guide and CreepyNC.com, detail the 1891 wreck's legend. While accounts vary somewhat, the man with the gold watch reportedly was first seen on the first anniversary.

According to CreepyNC.com, Hugh K. Linster was a baggage master for the Asheville-bound train that crashed into Third Creek that August of 1891.

"Hugh Linster never made it to retirement," the blog reads. "His body was found in the wreck having been killed immediately upon impact with a broken neck."

One year later, a group of people at the bridge said they saw a man in a railroad uniform, holding a watch.

He vanished before their eyes, legend has it (Gast).

THE MACO LIGHT

The story of the Maco light is fascinating and tragic. The source of the light is believed to be the spirit of Joe Baldwin, who died on the tracks near Maco, North Carolina.

In 1867, Joe was either a conductor or signalman for the Wilmington and Manchester Railroad. He was asleep in either a passenger car or the caboose when he was awakened by the jerk of the car he was in detaching from the rest of the train. Knowing that another train was due down those same tracks within minutes, Joe raced to try to signal it to stop before it collided with the runaway car.

Standing on the rear platform of the car, Joe grabbed his lantern and began swinging it wildly to signal to the other train's engineer that danger was ahead. His plan worked. The other engineer saw Joe's signal and immediately applied the brakes. Unfortunately for Joe, the speed of the oncoming passenger train was too great and it ultimately collided with his car and he was decapitated.

Because of Joe Baldwin's quick thinking and bravery, he saved many lives that night and was buried "with hero's honors" (The Maco Light). After that, mysterious lights were seen along the tracks near Maco Station near Wilmington and some have even claimed to have photographed them. It has been reported as well that "President Grover Cleveland saw the lights while on whistle stop tour in 1889" (The Maco Light). Those who have observed the strange phenomenon claim it is the ghost of Joe Baldwin warning of oncoming trains or searching for his head that was never recovered from the swamp. In 1977 the tracks were removed from Maco and the lights have not been reported since.

OHIO

THE ENGINEER'S GHOST

On December 29, 1876, a Pacific Express train with 109 passengers derailed while crossing a collapsed bridge. "Ninety people died, most of them burned alive while trapped inside the smashed cars" (Ashtabula County).

Reports indicate the ghosts of those who died that day can be seen below the bridge on the anniversary of the crash. Charles Collins who engineered the bridge committed suicide shortly after the crash. Amasa Stone, the designer of the bridge took his life a few years later. The ghost of Charles Collins has been seen at the memorial for the crash, reportedly leaning on it and crying. There are also reports of passengers from the crash being spotted in the nearby Chestnut Grove Cemetery.

RIVER STYX GHOST TRAIN

Many people have reported seeing the River Styx Ghost Train near the town of Medina, Ohio. Based on my research and that of others, the River Styx Ghost Train is actually near Rittman. I was just as disappointed as you are that there weren't two ghost trains, but it is better to have accurate information instead of pursuing wild ghost chases.

The town of Rittman was named after the treasurer of B&O Railroad, Fred Rittman. Early on March 22, 1899, the Erie Limited was westbound from Akron, when Engine No. 5's driving rod snapped. Engineer Alexander W. Logan attempted to reverse the train, but it derailed at the River Styx Trestle, approximately one mile east of the Rittman Depot. Everyone survived except Engineer Logan. "They found him in the wreckage, still clutching the throttle" (Summers).

Newspaper articles from 1900 to 1902 contain various reports of phantom trains along that stretch of track. The reports indicate the phantom train careens off of the tracks, "landing in a fiery inferno in the creek below" (Summers). One such report was in the Wooster Daily Republican on November 8, 1899. Wayne County Coroner, Dr. William Faber and his friend witnessed a phantom train plunge from a bridge. The train was covered in flames and Dr. Faber stated he heard the screams of people from inside. When they approached the wreckage, the train was gone (Wooster Daily Republican).

THE WAVING MAN

The Moonville tunnel is the result of the railroad. Built in the 1800's the tracks served as a shortcut to Cincinnati used to haul coal and clay. The narrow tunnel opened to a high trestle over a canyon. Some people opted to walk through the tunnel and over the trestle instead of going around. This shortcut led to the deaths of at least five people who were struck by oncoming trains, "...the most recent in 1986" (10).

Except for the ghostly activity, the tracks are abandoned. There are a few variations about the waving light seen inside the tunnel. One legend tells of a hard winter that led to a dangerous reduction in supplies. The trains would run through the town, but didn't stop. A man volunteered to stand inside the tunnel and wave a light in hopes of stopping the train. Unfortunately, he wasn't able to get out of the tunnel in time and was struck by the train.

Another variation involves a drunken man who tried to take the tunnel as a shortcut home. When he saw the train coming, he waved his lantern to let the engineer know he was in there. Again, the train was not stopped in time and the man was struck and killed.

It is believed that the waving man is still in the tunnel and his light can be seen as his ghost is still trying to get the attention of an oncoming train. It is rumored that the waving man's ghost caused such a stir the railroad company installed a signal light at the mouth of the tunnel and instructed engineers to ignore any lights they saw inside. Because the rails are abandoned, there is no way of officially knowing if this is accurate. The story of the waving man is so popular it "…has inspired songs, and there [is] even a novel about…a conductor that met an unfortunate fate there" (10). The novel is An Incident at Moonville: The Conductor's Revenge by William M. Cullen.

PENNSYLVANIA

HORSESHOE CURVE

In 1852 Irish laborers constructed Horseshoe Curve in Blair County between Johnstown and Altoona, Pennsylvania. The tracks there were designed by Edgar Thompson and built by the Pennsylvania Railroad. The system was later used by Penn Central and Conrail. It is now owned by the Norfolk Southern Railway and used by Amtrak's Pennsylvanian. "It [is] located in the Kittanning Gap at the summit of the Allegheny Mountains, five miles west of Altoona" (Ieraci).

Sightings of a young girl in white named Colleen have been reported on the Altoona side of the curve, just outside the tunnel. It is believed that she is waiting for the man she loves – a worker killed in a bar fight. According to John Hunter Orr, you can see Colleen by following these instructions:

> Drive up past the three reservoirs to the tunnel seven minutes before midnight. Arrive only on the night of a full moon.
>
> Proceed only when [precipitation is present]. Drive through the tunnel heading uphill.
>
> Turn around 50 yards on the other side using a pull-off. Face downhill with the car in neutral and the engine running. Be sure no other cars are present (obey traffic signals). Synchronize your watches. Keep totally silent. Begin the

drive forward entering the tunnel exactly at
midnight. Turn off your car lights as you enter.
(Do this at your own risk.) Drive slowly and
cautiously. Beep your horn three times in the
tunnel. Upon exiting the tunnel see immediately
on the right the young Irish lass in white. Look for
her sitting on the wall or standing by the first
spruce tree. If she is not there, look for her just
beyond where half a dozen other spruces stand
along a fence (Orr).

More impressive than the sightings of Colleen is the story of the
Red Arrow. On February 18, 1947 the Red Arrow, owned by the
Pennsylvania Railroad, jumped the tracks a few miles from
Horseshoe Curve, near Bennington Curve. "Eleven of fourteen
cars derailed; several tumbled down a 100 [foot] embankment.
[Twenty-four] people died in that wreck and another 131 were
injured" (Ieraci).

It is reported if you park near Gallitzen tunnel, which is
approximately one mile from the crash site, and flash your
headlights three times and shut off your car's engine, you will
hear voices talking and laughing followed by the appearance of
the ghosts making their way toward you.

The 1947 crash was not the last for the Red Arrow. In 1951 it
collided with another train, killing eight and injuring another 63

people. There have been no reports of ghostly activity as a result of that crash.

RHODE ISLAND

THE RICHMOND SWITCH DISASTER

Sometime during the mid-to-late 1800's Engineer Giles was driving his train near Providence, Rhode Island. A storm had caused a stream to swell, taking out the bridge near Providence and Stonington Road. That night, Engineer Giles did his best to save the train by putting the locomotive in reverse, but it was too late. His fireman jumped from the engine and survived. Giles was not so lucky.

The engine jumped the stream and crashed. "…they found Giles lying under his overturned engine with the lever driven through his body and one hand clutching the throttle valve with the grasp of death" (Clark).

Giles had a habit of signaling to his wife when he was returning to Providence with two blasts from the train's whistle. It was his way of telling her he would be home soon. After the accident, the engine was rebuilt, but the railroad had difficulty finding operators for it, due to superstitions.

To this day, people still report hearing two whistle blasts in the area; the ghost of Engineer Giles still signaling to his wife.

TEXAS

GHOST CHILDREN

San Antonio, Texas is home to one of the most notorious track hauntings in the U.S. South of the city, near the San Juan Mission at the intersection of Villamin and Shane are the famous ghost children tracks!

The legend tells of a tragic school bus accident in the 1930's or 40's. The bus was allegedly stalled on the tracks. The engineer saw the bus but was unable to stop in time. "Ten children reportedly lost their lives that day" (Weisen) and a grief-stricken nun is said to have taken her life a few days later.

It is said that the children protect the tracks at that intersection to prevent a recurrence of their fate. After dusting their back bumpers with flour or baby powder, witnesses claim their cars have been pushed *up*hill over the tracks after they've turned off the ignition. After crossing the tracks, they find what appear to be fingerprints in the powder – presumably from the ghosts of the children.

This unusual phenomenon has been covered by print media and television for decades. The one thing that investigators and media agree on is that there are no records of a train wreck or school bus accident having ever happened in that area. From there, the disagreements commence.

Most recently, the SyFy show Fact or Faked covered the story. They were able to effectively determine that the angle of the trees created an optical illusion; the hill appeared to be at an upward angle, when it was actually a two-degree downward angle. Vehicles in neutral were actually travelling downhill - the earth's gravitational pull moving them across the tracks. The mysterious fingerprints were actually a result of residual oils from the last time the vehicle was touched by the living. Using the powder enhances the fingerprints the same way law enforcement officials obtain fingerprints at crime scenes.

Some witnesses claim to hear the voices of children in the area as well. This can be attributed to the nearby residential areas. While this is an exciting location and thrill-seekers have visited it for years, extreme caution should be exercised when visiting this particular location. In recent years, investigators and thrill seekers alike have been attacked by purse-snatchers, car-jackers, and physical assaults have been reported. This lawlessness increases closer to Halloween. It has grown to such an extent that residents and law enforcement have grown weary of the area and aren't exceptionally friendly to investigators in the area.

DEAD MAN'S RUN

The events at Dead Man's Run in Sulphur Springs, Texas are notorious for residual ghostly activity. Taking place around 1890, the legend tells of a rail worker who was having marital troubles. He coerced his wife to accompany him to the tracks for a romantic rendezvous. Instead of the romance he had promised, he beat her severely and tied her to the tracks. Under the assumption she was unconscious, he sat next to her body to rest. Unbeknownst to him, she was very much conscious and stealthily tied his boot laces to the tracks. How she did this while tied to the tracks herself is a mystery, but that's how the legend goes.

Feeling guilty about what he had done to his love, he stayed with her on the tracks until he saw the train approaching. The man got up to leave, but found his laces fast secured to the tracks with several knots. He tried in vain to free himself, while his wife laughed. The man, along with his still-bound wife, was struck by the train and killed.

Witnesses claim that year-round you can sit on the deserted tracks and see a ball of light that resembles that of a locomotive headlight. No other activity has been reported other than the light and it remains in the distance. They also claim that on November 12 at approximately 3 a.m. a residual reenactment of the event occurs. It is said that at that moment "you can get out of your car and sit on the tracks and you will witness the entire scene. You can hear the man screaming and the woman laughing" (Deanna D.).

To access the tracks and check it out for yourself, drive down Highway 11 toward Commerce. Approximately two miles down the road, on the right-hand side you will see a small "oil-topped road" (Deanna D.). Take that road and follow it to the tracks.

UTAH

STEEDE'S POND

This location is bitter-sweet for me. I was very excited to discover it during my research for this book, but I am very disappointed that I didn't know of the ghostly activity until now. During my military service, I was stationed just minutes away and used to fish the pond regularly. There are no longer tracks next to Steede's Pond in Clearfield, Utah, but that doesn't take away from the ghostly activity.

"When those tracks were active, the stretch that runs the length of [Steede's Pond] was the deadliest in Utah. More people were hit and killed by trains on that stretch than anywhere else in Utah" (Chasing Kaos Paranormal). To add to the grisly area, several people drowned in the pond itself to include a boy who went for a swim one day after school.

The tracks were located on the eastern side of the pond. They have been removed and a paved walking path is now in their place, but there is still activity in the area to include shadow people, heavy feelings, wet footprints, people crying and calls for help.

VERMONT

THE HAUNTED TRESTLE

In 1887 a train wreck in Hartford, Vermont claimed the lives of several people and completely destroyed the wooden trestle that spanned the White River and Route 14.

Reports indicate the ghost of a small boy plays in the river at all times of the year. The boy is said to be the son of a man who died in the accident. It is possible that the boy had tried unsuccessfully to free his father from the wreckage. When he is spotted, he appears to be approximately one foot above the water.

Today a steel bridge spans the river and the road, utilizing the original stone pillars. People in the area of the bridge frequently report the smell of wood burning with no fire present, presumably from the original trestle when it went up in flames.

VIRGINIA

BIG BULL TUNNEL

Southwest Virginia's Big Bull Tunnel is located between St. Paul and Coeburn. An extension of the Norfolk & Western Railway, there are conflicting reports as to how many men have died in the tunnel. Two are known for sure, but some reports indicate a third man met his fate within the tunnel's walls. Reports of ghostly activity in the tunnel have been circulating for over one hundred years.

In July of 1905, N&W train men "began to witness or hear ghostly evidence, although the people living in the vicinity of the tunnel had claimed for years that the ghosts were in existence in the long tunnel through which the trains passed" (Branning). The most compelling of these stories took place on July 17 when a freight train broke down just outside the tunnel. Flagman, John Perry ran into the tunnel to place a warning on the other side to any approaching train, so as to avoid a collision. He never made it to the other side.

Trainmen Callaway and Kearns observed Perry burst from the tunnel's entrance and headed toward them at a dead run. "He had the appearance of a man who had been badly frightened" (Branning). Perry swore he had encountered a ghost, so Callaway and Kearns decided to follow him back into the tunnel. They wanted to see for themselves what had Perry so shaken.

Three men, if not more, had lost their lives in the tunnel. Conductor Hall, who assisted in arching the tunnel in 1903, swore it was haunted—or at least, the sounds heard were not subject to any explanation. Several trainmen made arrangements to investigate the ghost story further. The incident created a great deal of comments and excitement to those people residing near the tunnel (Branning).

Hikers can access the tunnel by taking Bull Run Road to Bull Hill Road and hiking to the tunnel from the road. Perhaps there is spirit activity today in Big Bull Tunnel. Maybe the legends are a bunch of bull…

WEST VIRGINIA

SCREAMING JENNY

The tale of Screaming Jenny is a popular one in West Virginia folklore. As with any good tale, there are conflicting stories, but the resulting ghostly activity is the same with this story.

The town of Duffields is located in Jefferson County, West Virginia, not far from Kearneysville. There is a small section of track, near the Harpers Ferry Station, that is famous for its resident ghost, Jenny of Duffields. How Jenny met her demise is where the stories conflict. One story claims "Jenny was running near the railroad tracks. She had just gotten word that her brand new husband had just been killed and as she ran screaming down the railroad tracks, she didn't see or hear the train coming and it ran over her and killed her" (Long).

The other story, believe it or not, is much more grisly. According to S.E. Schlosser:

> The old storage sheds along the tracks were abandoned shortly after the Baltimore & Ohio Railroad was built, and it wasn't long before the poor folk of the area moved in. The sheds provided shelter - of a sort - although the winter wind still pierced through every crevice, and the small fireplaces that the poor constructed did little to keep the cold at bay.

A gentle, kindly woman named Jenny lived alone in one of the smaller sheds. She had fallen on hard times, and with no family to protect her, she was forced to find work where she could and take whatever shelter was available to someone with little money. Jenny never had enough to eat and in winter her tiny fire barely kept her alive during the cold months. Still, she kept her spirits up and tried to help other folks when they took sick or needed food, sometimes going without herself so that another could eat.

One cold evening in late autumn, Jenny sat shivering over her fire, drinking broth out of a wooden bowl, when a spark flew from the fire and lit her skirts on fire. Intent on filling her aching stomach, Jenny did not notice her flaming clothes until the fire had burnt through the heavy wool of her skirt and began to scorch her skin. Leaping up in terror, Jenny threw her broth over the licking flames but the fluid did nothing to douse the fire. In terror, Jenny fled from the shack and ran along the tracks, screaming for help as the flames engulfed her body.

The station was not far away, and instinctively Jenny made for it, hoping to find someone to aid her. Within moments, her body was a glowing inferno and Jenny was overwhelmed by pain. Her screams grew more horrible as her steps slowed. She staggered blindly onto the tracks just west of the station, a ball of fire that barely looked human. In her agony, she did not see the glowing headlight of the train rounding the curve, or hear the screech of the breaks as the engineer spotted her fire-eaten figure and tried to stop. A moment later, her terrible screams broke off as the train mowed her down.

Alerted by the whistle, the crew from the station came running as the engineer halted the train and ran back down the tracks toward poor dead Jenny, who was still burning. The men doused the fire and carried her body back to the station. She was given a pauper's funeral and buried in an unmarked grave in the local churchyard. Within a few days, another poverty-stricken family had moved into her shack, and Jenny was forgotten. (Schlosser)

Over the years, many people have reported hearing the ghostly screams of Jenny in both the area of her old shed and on the tracks where she met her end. Train engineers claim to have seen Jenny's burning ghost on the tracks and have frantically stopped their trains, only to discover nothing on the tracks where they anticipated the body to be.

Is the residual energy that was Jenny of Duffields still running on the tracks? Maybe it's an intelligent haunting and she is still seeking to escape the flames? The shack where Jenny lived is now on private property, but the tracks are still accessible for anyone who wants to see for themselves!

SILVER RUN No. 19

The now ghost town of Silver Run, West Virginia is located in Ritchie County, near Cairo. The tracks that ran through Silver Run were owned by B&O. They had trains on them every hour but were abandoned in the 1980's. "It wasn't [uncommon] for them to hit someone on the tracks, usually a drunk who veered into the path of a speeding engine or someone committing suicide by train (Ieraci). There are many tales of ghosts resulting from such deaths.

The tracks near Silver Run tunnel No. 19 are notorious for ghostly activity, with one in particular – a lady in white. She was first spotted in the early 1900's. On an August night, it was nearing midnight as a train engineer was maneuvering his locomotive down the tracks near tunnel No. 19 when he "noticed a mist, and out of it emerged a young, distracted woman standing on the tracks with black hair and ghostly white skin, wearing a long, shadowy white gown. In a panic, he hit the brakes, but he knew that he couldn't miss the lady in white, who just turned and stared at the approaching engine" (Ieraci).

The engineer turned on his whistle to warn of the oncoming train to no avail. "At the moment the startled engineer thought that his train was about to slam into the woman, he watched her fly up into the air only to disappear into the night" (Ghost of Silver Run).

The engineer used every ounce of strength he had to control his train as he brought it to a stop. He was certain he had hit the woman and imagined the horrific sight that awaited him once they stopped.

> The engineer and his crew searched for a corpse, assuming that [hitting her had] sent her body flying through the air, but none was found. Writing it off to a hallucination caused by tired eyes and dancing headlights, they finished the run.

> [sic] In the following weeks, the same event would sporadically play out, usually during a half moon. The engineer passed on his story and the B&O officials transferred him to a different line (Ieraci).

A veteran engineer named O'Flannery was assigned the run. He was a skeptic and put absolutely no weight into the story of the woman haunting tunnel No. 19. "O'Flannery wouldn't have any of it. He laughed with bitter sarcasm and vowed that no ghost was going to stop his train – he'd run her down first" (Ghost of Silver Run).

As fate would have it, Engineer O'Flannery encountered the mysterious woman the same night he started the route. Arriving at the Silver Run Station, he recounted the story of his encounter, but was told by B&O officials that "he'd lose his job if he too was going to [relay] stories of a spooked-out tunnel" (Ieraci).

O'Flannery decided then and there that he would definitely run the woman over the next time he saw her. He wasn't about to risk his livelihood or his reputation for that matter. Naturally, the engineer did see the woman again. Determined to not let the ghost get the best of him, he maintained his speed and drove the train straight through her.

> By this time, O'Flannery was, in fact, unnerved. Sweat poured from his brow. He felt tremendously relieved to get his train through the Silver Run Tunnel. Even so, O'Flannery was still a boastful type who looked forward to bragging about how he ran the Ghost of Silver Run down to the other engineers. Later, as the Irishman pulled into the 6th Street train station in Parkersburg, O'Flannery noticed the place was in a bit of a panic bordering on bedlam. As he walked through the door, he asked another engineer "Hey—what's all the commotion about?" The engineer answered,

> "Man, don't you know? You hit a woman at the Silver Run Tunnel and she rode all the way into Parkersburg on your cow catcher!"

O'Flannery was left uncharacteristically
speechless. After all, the spirit had made a
mockery of the man as she would many doubters
to come.

Apparently, earlier in the evening, calls flooded
the 6th Street train station in Parkersburg from
smaller stations along the rails [reporting] a thinly
dressed woman was riding the cow catcher of
O'Flannery's engine…As soon as the engine
[arrived] at the 6th Street Station, the woman
vanished (Ghost of Silver Run).

Engineer O'Flannery immediately requested a transfer and, given
the circumstances of that night, it was granted with no questions
asked. B&O began in investigation into Silver Run Tunnel No.
19. They discovered that "25 years prior, a woman in a white
gown had ridden the train to Silver Run to meet her fiancé and
get married. She disappeared after leaving the train" (Ieraci).

Many suspected this woman to be the ghost that was plaguing the
tracks of Tunnel No. 19. "In the 1940's, the skeleton of a woman,
still dressed in white shreds, was found stuffed in the chimney of
a long deserted home on the outskirts of town. She was given a
proper church burial, and after that, she seemed at peace and the
lady in white faded into legend" (Ieraci).

Before that, many B&O engineers claimed to have encountered the Ghost of Silver Run. Today, the occasional bicyclist will report hearing a train whistle inside the tunnel and locals still claim that on clear nights during the half-moon a thinly-clad ghost can be seen floating down the tracks just outside Silver Run Tunnel No. 19.

BIBLIOGRAPHY

10 Haunted Tunnels With Really Creepy Backstories - Listverse. (n.d.). Retrieved from http://listverse.com/2014/02/11/10-haunted-tunnels-with-really-creepy-backstories/

Ashtabula County Hauntings & Legends. (n.d.). Retrieved from http://www.ohioexploration.com/ashtabulacounty.htm

Avon Railroad Tracks | Haunted Places | Avon, Iowa. (n.d.). Retrieved from http://www.hauntedplaces.org/item/avon-railroad-tracks/

Branning, D. (2012, August 3). Ghost of Big Bull Tunnel in Virginia - National Haunted Places | Examiner.com. Retrieved from http://www.examiner.com/article/ghost-of-big-bull-tunnel-virginia

Bybee, J. D. (2013, May 6). Rain, Wind, and Woe: The Flatwoods Ghost Train, Part 1 – Mysterious Heartland. Retrieved from http://mysteriousheartland.com/2013/05/06/rain-wind-and-woe-the-flatwoods-ghost-train-part-1/

Chasing Kaos Paranormal. (n.d.). Haunted Location: Steeds Pond
| Chasing Kaos. Retrieved from
http://www.chasingkaos.com/haunted-location-steeds-
pond/

Clark, J. (2005). *Unnatural phenomena: A guide to the bizarre
wonders of North America.* Santa Barbara, CA: Abc-clio.

Davies, D. (n.d.). The Legend of the Lincoln Ghost Train
Hudson Valley Halloween Magazine. Retrieved from
http://www.hudsonvalleyhalloweenmagazine.com/haunte
d-hudson-valley/lincoln-ghost-train

Deanna D. (2012, March 30). Dead Man's Run. Retrieved from
http://deannad97.hubpages.com/hub/Dead-Mans-Run

Durwin, J. (2006, November 23). These Mysterious Hills:
December 2006. Retrieved from http://mysterious-
hills.blogspot.com/2006_12_01_archive.html

Elmhurst, Illinois, Ghost Sightings. (n.d.). Retrieved from
http://www.ghostsofamerica.com/6/Illinois_Elmhurst_gho
st_sightings4.html

Florence and Cripple Creek Railroad - Wikipedia, the free
encyclopedia. (n.d.). Retrieved October 19, 2014, from
http://en.wikipedia.org/wiki/Florence_and_Cripple_Creek
_Railroad

Funeral and Burial of Abraham Lincoln - Wikipedia, the free
encyclopedia. (n.d.). Retrieved October 22, 2014, from
http://en.wikipedia.org/wiki/Funeral_and_burial_of_Abrah
am_Lincoln

Gast, P. (2010, August 28). 'Ghost train' hunter killed by train in
North Carolina - CNN.com. Retrieved from
http://www.cnn.com/2010/US/08/27/north.carolina.ghost.t
rain/

Ghost Legends of Indiana - Wikipedia, the free encyclopedia.
(n.d.). Retrieved October 21, 2014, from
http://en.wikipedia.org/wiki/Ghost_legends_of_Indiana

Ghost Train (folklore) - Wikipedia, the free encyclopedia. (n.d.).
Retrieved October 22, 2014, from
http://en.wikipedia.org/wiki/Ghost_train_(folklore)

Haunt in railroad tracks Tolono, Illinois is haunted! Haunted
places in Tolono, IL (Illinois) from Hauntings. (n.d.).
Retrieved from http://v3.hauntin.gs/railroad-
tracks_Tolono_Illinois_United-States_4184

Haunted places in Georgia. (n.d.). Retrieved from
http://www.hauntedhovel.com/hauntedplacesingeorgia.ht
ml

Haunted Places in Lake Charles, LA. (n.d.). Retrieved from
http://www.hauntedplaces.org/lake-charles-la/

Headless Brakeman: A Ghostly Apparition That Haunts a

Siding and Brings Disaster. (1894, June 15). *Syracuse Sunday Herald*. Retrieved from http://www.bellaterreno.com/art/a_newspaper/news_ghost _brakeman.aspx

Hilkevitch, J. (2013, October 1). CTA: Video shows no one at

controls of train before collision - Chicago Tribune. Retrieved from http://articles.chicagotribune.com/2013- 10-01/news/chi-two-cta-trains-crash-on-blue-line-in- forest-park-20130930_1_runaway-train-train-operator-cta- rail-workers-union

Hilkevitch, J. (2013, November 1). 2 fired, 2 suspended in CTA

'ghost train' crash - Chicago Tribune. Retrieved from http://articles.chicagotribune.com/2013-11-01/news/chi-2- fired-2-suspended-in-cta-ghost-train-crash- 20131101_1_cta-spokesman-brian-steele-cta-rules-cta- rail-workers-union

History.Com Staff. (2009). *Abraham Lincoln's Funeral Train –*

Facts & Summary - HISTORY.com [Video file]. Retrieved from http://www.history.com/topics/president-lincolns- funeral-train

Hookerman Lights, New Jersey. (n.d.). Retrieved from

http://usersites.horrorfind.com/home/ghosts/hauntedus/hoo kerman.htm

Ieraci, R. (n.d.). Pennsylvania Haunts & History: Spooks of the
Curve. Retrieved from
http://hauntsandhistory.blogspot.com/2009/05/spooks-of-
curve.html

Ieraci. (n.d.). Pennsylvania Haunts & History: The Legend of
Silver Run's Lady In White. Retrieved from
http://hauntsandhistory.blogspot.com/2010/06/legend-of-
silver-runs-lady-in-white.html

Kate Shelly High Bridge | Haunted Places | Boone, Iowa. (n.d.).
Retrieved from http://www.hauntedplaces.org/item/kate-
shelly-high-bridge/

Keipp, L. (n.d.). Ghostly trains and haunted rails: the ghost train
of Marshall Pass - Denver History | Examiner.com.
Retrieved from http://www.examiner.com/article/ghostly-
trains-and-haunted-rails-the-ghost-train-of-marshall-pass

Long, R. (2004, July 14). Screaming Jenny Of Duffields – West
Virginia Ghosts. Retrieved from
http://www.wvghosts.com/archives/674

Lost Locomotive of Kiowa Creek | National Underwater and
Marine Agency. (n.d.). Retrieved from
http://www.numa.net/expeditions/lost-locomotive-of-
kiowa-creek/

Martin, Mary Joy. Phantoms of the Rails - Deadly Engine 107 |

   GORP.com. (n.d.). Retrieved from
   http://www.gorp.com/weekend-guide/travel-ta-historic-
   railroads-colorado-sidwcmdev_056595.html

(1899, November 8). *Wooster Daily Republican*. Print.

Odd Places, Travels and Spooks of Mile-High: Haunted Colorado

   Locations. (n.d.). Retrieved from
   http://coloradoghosts.blogspot.com/2010/02/haunted-
   colorado-locations.html

Orr, J. H. (n.d.). The Secret Irish Pennsylvania Ghost. Retrieved

   from http://www.pennsylvania-mountains-of-
   attractions.com/pennsylvania-ghost.html

Railroad tracks Tolono, Il 61880 Champaign County Haunt.

   (n.d.). Retrieved from
   http://www.strangeusa.com/ViewLocation.aspx?id=3133
   &Description=_railroad_tracks__Tolono__IL

RootsWeb: FOLKLORE-L [FOLKLORE-L] Haunted Railroad

   Trestle. (1999, June 26). Retrieved from
   http://archiver.rootsweb.ancestry.com/th/read/FOLKLOR
   E/1999-06/0930426336

Schlosser, S. E. (n.d.). Ghost on the Tracks: From Ghost Stories at

Americanfolklore.net. Retrieved from
http://americanfolklore.net/folklore/2010/07/ghost_on_the
_tracks.html

Schlosser, S. E. (n.d.). Phantom Train Wreck: From Ghost Stories
at Americanfolklore.net. Retrieved from
http://americanfolklore.net/folklore/2010/07/the_phantom
_train_wreck.html

Schlosser, S. E. (n.d.). Screaming Jenny: From Scary stories at
Americanfolklore.net. Retrieved from
http://americanfolklore.net/folklore/2010/07/screaming_je
nny.html

Schlosser, S. E. (2004). *Spooky Southwest: Tales of hauntings,
strange happenings, and other local lore*. Guilford, CT:
Globe Pequot Press.

Schlosser, S. E. (2006). The Express Train to Hell. In *Spooky New
Jersey: Tales of hauntings, strange happenings, and other
local lore*. Guilford, CT: Insiders' Guide.

Shadowlands Haunted Places Index - Colorado. (n.d.). Retrieved
from http://www.theshadowlands.net/places/colorado.htm

Southern Indiana Ghosts-Danville Indiana Haunted Bridge. (n.d.).
Retrieved from
http://www.angelfire.com/in4/believe/danvillebridge/danvi
llebridge.html

Summers, K. (2011, September 29). The Hunt for Ohio State's River Styx Ghost Train by Ken Summers. Retrieved from http://www.ghostvillage.com/resources/2011/features_092 92011.shtml

Taylor, T. (1998). White Lick Creek Bridge / Haunted Indiana. Retrieved from http://www.prairieghosts.com/dan.html

The Ghost of Silver Run. (n.d.). Retrieved from http://users.wirefire.com/magick/new_page_9.htm

The Haunted Railroad Bridge Hartford, Vt 05047 Windsor County Haunt. (n.d.). Retrieved from http://www.strangeusa.com/ViewLocation.aspx?id=10199 &Description=_The_Haunted_Railroad_Bridge__Hartford __Vt

The Maco Light | North Carolina Ghost Stories and Legends. (n.d.). Retrieved from http://www.northcarolinaghosts.com/coast/maco-light.php

The Phantom Train of Marshall Pass by Charles M. Skinner. (n.d.). Retrieved from http://www.legendsofamerica.com/co-marshallpass.html

Train Wreck Dumas, Mo Clark Haunt. (n.d.). Retrieved from http://www.strangeusa.com/ViewLocation.aspx?id=5859 &Description=_Train_Wreck__Dumas__Mo

Tupaczewski, P. (n.d.). Hookerman Lights, New Jersey. Retrieved

    from http://usersites.horrorfind.com/home/ghosts/haunted

    us/tupaczewski.htm

Vazquez, Clarissa (2011). *Ghost Hunting in Colorado: Theories*

    for World-Wide Investigators. Self Published.

Weird Texas. (n.d.). Retrieved from

    http://www.weirdus.com/states/texas/road_less_traveled/c

    hildren_of_the_tracks/index.php

Weiser, K. (2010). Ghostly Children upon San Antonio's Railroad

    Tracks. Retrieved from

    http://www.legendsofamerica.com/tx-ghostlychildren.html

Whichter, T. (2012, July 6). Helvetica's Indie Horror Stories:

    Haunted Adrian, Michigan. Retrieved from

    http://helveticasindiehorrorstories.blogspot.com/2012/07/h

    aunted-adrian-michigan.html

William Wallace Lincoln - Wikipedia, the free encyclopedia.

    (n.d.). Retrieved October 22, 2014, from

    http://en.wikipedia.org/wiki/William_Wallace_Lincoln

Your Guide to the supernatural: Louisiana. (n.d.). Retrieved from

    http://www.ghosttraveller.com/louisiana.htm

Clarissa Vazquez is a Colorado native and avid paranormal investigator, having founded the Colorado Coalition of Paranormal Investigators (CCPI) in 2004. She has written several books on ghosts and the paranormal to include *Ghosts of the Heart: A Paranormal Investigator's Journey, Ghost Hunting in Colorado: Theories for World-Wide Investigators Demons of the Coven, and No Monsters Here!* In addition to her own literary works, Clarissa has been a featured author in books such as *Picture Yourself Capturing Ghosts on Film*, by Christopher Balzano, *Ghosts from Coast to Coast*, by Kalyomi, and Ghosts *of Colorado*, by Dennis Baker.

She is most noted for her paranormal research and development of the Phantom Hitchhiker Project – designed to prove that paranormal investigation *can* be conducted scientifically and thus should be recognized as legitimate research by the mainstream scientific community.

Clarissa has been featured on terrestrial and Internet radio shows alike to include *Coast to Coast A.M.* with George Noory, *Spooky Southcoast* with Tim Weisberg, and *Darkness on the Edge of Town* with David Schrader. You can find her hosting *Para-Scope Uncensored* every Friday night on the Hey-Z Radio Network.